She Wears Him Fancy in Her Night Braid

SHE WEARS HIM FANCY
IN HER NIGHT BRAID

"The heart *is* deceitful above all things,
and desperately wicked; who can know it."
Jeremiah, 17:9

The Toothpaste Press :: West Branch, Iowa

Some of these poems have appeared in the following magazines, anthologies, small presses: *HardPressed, I Hear My Sisters Saying, Ironwood, waves, Handbook, Sailing the Air Clear,* University of Arizona *Poetry Center* newsletter, and as part of 500 original poemcards for the Alternative Press. Part 7 appeared as a broadside published by the Midwestern Writers' Festival, 1980.

The artist wishes to express her gratitude to the art of: Jean-Baptiste-Simeon Chardin, Joseph Cornell, Leonardo da Vinci, Michelangelo, the sea shells of David Bornstein, Signorelli, Lennart Nilsson, *Wisconsin Death Trip,* Bantam *Knowledge through Color* series.

The Poliphilus and Goudy Open types were handset by A. B. & David Duer. Allan Kornblum designed and printed 1,475 copies, all on Simpson Gainsborough text. The author has signed 75 numbered copies, quarter-bound in cloth & Japanese paper over boards.

Library of Congress CIP Data

Kicknosway, Faye.
   She wears him fancy in her night braid.

I. Title.
PS3561.I32S45 1983   811'.54   83-18272
ISBN 0-915124-88-2
ISBN 0-915124-87-4 (pbk.)

In memory of my teacher, Sheldon Tannenbaum,
and of my good friend, Robert Ridley.

I

They come and go,
walk through my mind, my heart, shiny
until I touch them: rubber bands, pinochle cards.
I blame my stars, my life, my knees, my smile.
I blame the potatoes on the stove, the toast,
the tea. Myself. Sunshine walks toward me
I want to taste to the roots
of my hair

and I reach my hand out
and sweat jumps
I forget to breathe and blink
my heart salivates
it all turns over:
color is what my arms feel even through shirt sleeves,
my lips and tongue see.
Love:
it is a tonic I drink with my senses.
It is molasses. Sassafras.

2

I dance long and large
and the man in my memory

bristles
to the ends of his moustache.
I wheel
dark as memory
call
him real.

Michael,
of the visible moon
air wet
shadows fat and juicy.
His marvelous weight
desire to enter.

So much politeness
and he was going to wash my hair
take my shoes off
as soon as he figured out how
to do it
without touching me.

He was camphor and tea cosies
made from porcelain
so delicate
breathing at him cracked him
walking too heavy in the next room
gave him stomach cramps.

Being in love with him
was like being in love with a lace curtain
or a puffball.

He came toward me, three-dimensional.
I looked at him, my eyes soft,
blue muzzles.
Closer,
grinning. He jumped past
my eyes so fast I thought him real.

I took the Moon from my pocket,
it ovulating.
He thought it fat, nasty
would not speak to it
until it got better.

Silence slept at my door.
He sent me telegrams, describing the moisture
in his heart. Stars were figs he shook
from the clear air.
And he wanted to fuck them,
to put his head on their breasts.

I was moon-struck, pale
a mouth, perfectly balanced
and fat elbows, watching nothing.

He,
the one picked up,
the one picked out,
needing big, round bandages to make him work,
rose up,
humid,
from the sky's cooking pot,

the cannibal, dark as stars.

I desired to swallow him, his nonchalance
and dimples.
I was lint in his pocket,
no entry into God.

And the day bloomed with flowers
the room grew itself new
and he,
eyes of many colors,
lay dreaming his sex loose and large,
cum hot on his belly.

A face without response
he walked from Sargeant Street,
from Madonnas and chestnuts,
from a father shooting pigeons.

Polak. Slav.
Immigrant, new man to this country.
My mother baked him bread.
My grandmother wore him fancy in her night
braid.

Sex was dark clothes, foreign, rose up
he thought
to bite him.
He would not open toward me,
but recited *Old Maid, Kick the Can,*
ritual games that are played
across a table,
across a street.

Distance was the song
he sang me. And I was Goldilocks,
alone, rhyming
on my fingers. He walked out

among the flowers,
ate them. His fingers were harps.
Fur; o,

the colors
he made. I felt
invisible.

3

My hair tangled and around
his face, in the corners
of his mouth.

"I could be anyone; you haven't
any feeling. I know what
I am to you."

He kept a calendar, notched
it, called me up
when I was safe.

"At least look at me."
"I am looking at you."
He rested his elbows
on the table,

the coffee cup warm
in his hands and moving up
toward his lips.

"You don't even know
who I am."
"Sure I do."

"Then say my name."
"Rabbit warren," he said,
"Notch in a tree. You're
 in a bad

 mood today; I think I'll see
 you later."

 Daylight. Birds
 fluttered up the sky.
 I stood at the window.

"Make no sexual energy."

"You're like some Goddamn, old-
 world fellow."

"I like to walk in the front door
 and have you handle
 me."

"You always laugh; it's like
 a threat; all things that can lead
 to you, you've put away."

"I'm your legacy, remember?
 The man who's been simmering

at the back of the stove,
getting warmed up
and dangerous.''

4

I am an anus.
Desirable. I talk plenty and am
devastating
when oral. I can piss loud enough
to crack walls open.
I hum semen,
an old myth manifested from thoughts
of him.
He is the payment I desire.

His cock is bare
and emerging.
''Romanticize yourself again,'' I say.
And he does. His spoor
is acceptable and intelligent.
It leaps out
clean
and hairy.

He is satisfied

and urinates. "To make the flowers
grow," he says,

but it's trees
he's after, tall
and old, controlled by miracles
and breathing.

My ducts
are loathsome. Do not emit me well
at all. He uses scissors
and paste.
"You are the wrong
activity," he says,

and in the morning, when
everything, even the breakfast table,
is empty,
and we must speak
to one another, the night

would be a good curtain
to hold between us. We both wish it.

"It is time to piss," he says.
"The toilet is in that direction," I say.
It is a symbolic separation.

I turn on the gas, the water, separate
the spoons
from the forks, think
of other times.

"O, I was a bottom once," I think,
"So good to touch. O,

I was a bottom once,
and I allowed it all."

5

I keep talking 'Michael',
on the bus,
outloud and laughing;
I know all the jokes.

Animals jump out of my head,
my hands, and squat
like people
around me.

I watch them,
say nothing. Sometimes I sleep

sitting up, in corsets and stays,
painful.
My sweat gets buttery on my collar,
my stockings,
my britches.

I get the angers,
the fits,
the leave-me-alones.
I swear and stomp,
but it does no good.
Nothing moves or changes.

I use the radio,
my feet, the sweat on my teeth
to distract myself.

He is the wrong tense,
the wrong film,
the wrong odor.

He was my fish, my flower.
Stars were shadows—such a long
time ago—he trapped me, drove me carefully
heavily
backward.

I was captive,
winter-stiffened.
He carried me in his teeth
from room to room.

What could I do?
He jumped
crab-footed,
thirsty,
hungry,
back and forth through me.

6

I am the woman of sweaty language, the belly
woman, the thigh woman.
I am the dunce, the maker of deliberate
magic, the obedient, the harmed.

I make the sky
perfect.
I put the stars in their sockets.

Loving him is whist and aspirin.
There is no country to it
nor city

nor anything held long enough
for a good look.

I want to hear
the metaphor of a porch swing, its wood,
the house creaking, lovers broken open,
visible.

I want this air
this dreamless air
let loose.

He limits me;
I am a pet: sit, beg.
He tells me I'm kind of nice
to have around.

He is the season of lilac.
Disease.

He sleeps.
I stand up, full of teeth,
scorned,
put aside.

My hair is white with anger.
There is fire in my legs.

I am dark,
the woman of gypsy people, the beggar,
fortune teller.
I am a gesture of hands, voice.
He lies with me
because I invite it,
I speak it.

I will not be ashen.
I will not be stitched
in the seam of an outside pocket.

Let him limit his cat,
his coat hangers,
the size of his footprints.
Let him limit dust.

7

And he is linen
he is
and he is roses
he is
and chairs
and scenes hand-painted
he is

and he is empty
when I hold him
he is
and he talks
and I listen
on walks in the morning
I'm older
I am
and I hide in the bushes
he looks at the ceiling
he does
and he tells me
be lonely
I am
come sit in his window
protect him
I do
he dreams
he is captive
and stone and grey curtains
shapeless
he is

8

I begin smoking.

My metabolism changes. My hands
sweat.
I am glued to myself.

Goodbye. Goodbye.
The smoke his hair, his eyes.

Goodbye.

''Let's fall in love;
why shouldn't we
fall in love?'' Twelve years old, the dream
entering my hair, I walked
somnambulent,
barefoot
past signboards, farmer's fields.
Dream.
Love dream,
somewhere in the air,
waiting to crack loose
as a whole person,
a right

person.
Twelve years old, in 2nd-hand,
3rd-hand, countrywoman dreams
steamed from laundry, from pots

at the back of the stove, from weather
wet as anger
heating up the road, love

dreams, lover

dreams brought up on a truck
from farmlands,
brought up tucked safe
in moon⁄wet eyes.
Goats, chickens, geese
have disappeared;
the dining room table and the cool,
half⁄light under it
has disappeared.

Mr. Perfect:
do
right: dust; bake;
keep myself still and he's
mine. The Promise.
He's walking up my blood
and I 'll blink him from my eyes
into the street,
into the passage the truck makes

toward my new home

in the city.
He licks my spit from his fingers,
blinks my sweat
from the corners of his eyes.
He'll bake me like bread in his long,
hard
arms. His smell is in me and he'll find
me like a ewe finds its lamb.
I'll float in him like he was tea
and I was sugar.
I dream him, eyes

tightly closed and arms hugged
around my body.
I dream him until the stones at the side
of the road glow, until the sky
flakes and cracks
like a painted plate,
the dusty trees sweat, houses
and barns lean down from the pressure
of him
walking toward me.

And I'd stir him in my flesh.
Timid.
Afraid mother'd
catch me.

Father'd see me. Afraid
he'd come loose
on my fingers.

9

I dreamed a man with eyes
like red agates stood
at the door.
He told me I made his socks
go up and down.
His name was Captain
and he missed me. His touch
scorched and I ran

to hide in a photograph
of Mother.

She was eating weeds
and smoke and cursed me,
her hairpins scattering
like cockroaches
across the walls
and chairs.

"He called himself Captain,"

I told her.
"Captain?"
"Yes."

"Captain," she said,
"I've missed you." She held
her hands out
toward me, then pressed
them against her skirt,
lifting it.
"Your little knicknack,
your little bead;
I've missed you."

I O

Luscious, sexual eyes
hand-sewn by Mother, he was

warm skin: silk,
cotton.

He was consummation,
my gypsy name.
Dangerous. Wolves

quiet in the snow, the tribe
Michael
gathers. Dark, hair and eyes.
Unknown to Christ
or His priests.

Daylight. In their pocket,
a foreign god, wrapped in skins:
angel

with fire wings
and Paradise at his back.
His sword burned like their sacred tree.

Michael.

I recognize him
in an old book of census
my great-grandmother kept,
pasting in recipes, poems
and the history

of her family.
Predator,

he walks from its pages,
becoming

cooper, gunsmith, striker.
He boards the ship 'America'
in 1683, a summer passage,
children sweaty and sick, the ocean
calm.

He is Frenchman, Huguenot,
and disembarks
in Philadelphia. The woman

he will marry
scrubs
her mother's kitchen floor

and dreams of love.
Her mother warns her: Pleasure

is the Devil's own
and has no place
in a young girl's life.

Nor in a wife's.
Nor in a mother's.

The love dream simmers
and brews
and daughters

peek
their noses in,

and are afraid to breathe
or sweat
for fear
of losing him, the dream-

man each
spoons
from the hot cauldron
of her mother's
heart.

II

I sit clumsy in my flesh, my legs
stiff, thick. I am
gemstones, collapsed and dried,
the magic bean nobody
wanted. I am the size of
grief. I am quiet and left
to sit with cats and
stoves and dripping faucets.
My socks dry on the bathroom rack.
The heat clicks on. It is pale in here

and nothing moves.
The silence of photographs.
The silence of snow. No one comes here except
by telephone.

I have been blind, blind. Drunk
on my own flesh.
Circumstance and habit were cloth mended to me
by hands
buried in the wallpaper
of houses I only visited
in dreams.

It begins.
My family coming loose as little pictures.
And they watch me.
And they are mostly dead.
And I
look backward into them as though they were tunnels.

It begins.

12

I am my mother's coffin,
and she rises up, small

and furious, on stilts
that clatter
and tap
beneath her.

Her wide ragged skirts
invade and dominate
the room, tumbling lamps
from tables, scaring mice

back
into their holes
in the floorboards
or into their nests
in the furniture ticking.

Her gloomy, dour little face
is knotted up and she pokes
and prods, tugs
and pushes, lifting
things up
to see beneath them.

She whirls
and the force of her movement
lifts the furniture,

the lamps and books,
figurines and rugs, up
into the air.

She scratches and tears;
pieces of sheet and curtain,
tablecloth and stocking
fly
from her fingers.

"He's not here," she whines,
and her unhappiness
shrinks her, and she collapses,
her tiny, bald head
sinking into the webs
and dust
her skirts have become.

"Go look up the chimney,"
I tell her. "Maybe he's there
in the soot
and ashes.
Can you see him?"

She lifts her head,
struggles
to free herself

from her skirts.

"Maybe that's him
at the gate," I tell her.
"Go look out the screen door.
Can you see
his dimples?
Do you recognize
his hips
and his shoulders?"